Preventing Workplace Burnout

Geary Reid

ISBN: 978-976-8305-64-0

ISBN: 978-976-8305-64-0

Acknowledgments

Great thanks must be expressed to the following people:

The heavenly Father, for granting me the wisdom and inspiration to record the information in this book, which I began on September 29, 2021, and completed on October 5, 2021; my family, for their continued encouragement and support regarding various challenges; and several people who have assisted with reviewing and editing the book:

- Shawn Rogers, Adv. Dipl. Project Mgmt., A+ Certification, Telecommunication Certification
- Judah Louisy, MSc, ACCA, FCPA
- Wonnette Nicholson, Dipl. in Business Management and Administration

To you, the reader: have fun while reading, and grasp and practice what you learn so that this world will become a better place. Many people are depending on your guidance. We all need a shoulder to lean on and a hand to guide us.

Geary Reid
MBA, FCCA, FAAPM, MPM, CAT

Reid's Learning Institute and Business Consultancy

reidnlearn.com

Amazon: amazon.com/author/gearyreid

Facebook: Reid n Learn

Instagram: Reid n Learn

LinkedIn: Reid's Learning Institute
and Business Consultancy

199 Kuru - Kururu, Soesdyke Linden Highway
Guyana, South America

Table of Contents

Introduction

Too many employees suffer from workplace burnout, and they do not always know how to identify and prevent it. Leaders often ask certain employees to do more without recognizing that they may be pushing those employees beyond their limits. When an employee becomes burnt out, not only does that employee suffer, but the organization may not be able to benefit in the same way from that employee. Employees are human, and they cannot be compared with machines, nor can they be given the same volume of work as machines to be completed with the same speed and accuracy. Even machines deserve rest.

Learning what contributes to workplace burnout is a good starting point for employees and employers, and this literature addresses many of the reasons for workplace burnout, some of which are very common. Leaders may not see all of these reasons as significant, and thus, when employees are pushed beyond their limit, they are unable to be effective for the organization.

Employees can become tired of doing the same job for lengthy periods, so they sometimes lose focus. Employers must seek to rotate those employees so that they will still have a desire to help the organization. The need to train and develop employees must be considered, since employees who are trained may develop skills to become more effective in their duties. Succession planning helps employees to know that their leaders care about them and may have the intention to promote them sometime soon.

To prevent workplace burnout, leaders must manage the amount of overtime work their employees do. Some employees will often want to work overtime, not recognizing that they need to rest their bodies. Annual vacation is important for all employees. While some employees may not always want to take their vacation on time, leaders must encourage their employees to do so, so that those employees will be rejuvenated and return to the organization refreshed. Employees will become ill from time to time, so a sick leave policy must be in place for them to utilize.

Acquiring Information Systems and Information Technology is a good investment for organizations to make, and it will reduce the possibility of workplace burnout. With the use of such systems and technology, more work may be completed in less time, and the leaders will have consistent quality outputs. Upgrading machines and equipment can also reduce workplace burnout.

Leaders have to balance the amount of work allocated to their employees to ensure that each employee has a balanced workload. Reviewing work regularly is important to reduce errors in the delivery of products and services to customers. If possible, employers can encourage and facilitate Medical Insurance schemes for employees to join and receive medical benefits if they suffer from workplace burnout.

1. Workplace burnout is real

Some persons think that once employees are paid, they must work throughout the whole day, every day. Many persons work for long hours under much strain and are counting the days until they will proceed on vacation, while others are thinking of when they will retire.

While employment provides persons with the opportunity to earn, leaders of every organization must remember that their employees are humans and must be given time to rest. The work some employees do is very strenuous, and therefore, their employers must consider investing in types of machinery and technologies to produce the same results.

1.1 Manual systems

While technology is available to help many organizations to increase their productivity, some organizations still lag in their use of technology or even still operate a manual system. Such organizations can be very labor intensive, and employees have to work under strenuous conditions daily.

When most of the work that employees have to do is manual, they may become tired, and while they want to take some rest, they may have to continue working until the tasks are completed.

1.2 Poor leadership

Sometimes, as a result of poor leadership, employees become burnt out. Leaders must be able to coordinate the resources that they have and make the best use of those resources, while at the same time preserving their human capital. Leaders must prioritize the distribution of the workload. If the workload is not properly distributed, then some employees will be overworked, while others may be underworked.

Overtime hours may be incurred to complete some urgent work. However, most employees should not be working overtime regularly, since their performance soon declines.

1.3 Little or no enforcement of vacation policy

In organizations that do not have a vacation policy, employers must consider creating one, as employees are entitled to some rest. Employees must be given some time away from the office so that they will remain effective for the organization.

In the absence of a vacation policy, employees may overwork. Some employers are happy when their employees are working almost every day, but that can become dangerous, since humans are expected to take some rest after hard work.

For those organizations that do have a vacation policy, leaders must enforce the policy by ensuring that employees proceed on vacation periodically. When some employees are on vacation, it provides other employees with the opportunity to perform different duties and develop their skills.

1.4 Few skilled employees

Some leaders want to keep their employment costs very low. However, if a small number of employees have to complete many tasks in a limited amount of time, they will experience burnout. Many employees become skilled at what they are doing, especially if they are doing the same job for a lengthy period and they like it. However, leaders must assess the workforce and not cause the few employees to become burnt out.

Employing a few more employees may prevent workplace burnout and, at the same time, enable the organization to meet the customers' demands. Whenever a few employees are constantly working beyond their normal hours, there is a possibility that those employees will make mistakes, and those mistakes may go undetected, since there may not be anyone to review their work.

1.5 Limited investment in types of machinery and advanced technology

While leaders may think that it takes too much money to invest in types of machinery and advanced technology, they must not overwork their employees. The absence of machinery may cause employees to constantly work long hours to meet customers' demands. However, when machines are acquired, they can easily complete some of the work that would otherwise be done by employees.

Information Technology and Information Systems are there to help organizations to complete their work and to deliver accurate and timely outputs. Information Systems can eliminate duplication of work, as they can retain data for a very long time and allow leaders to make strategic decisions. When employees are away from work, leaders do not have to contact them for information, since it will be easily available through the Information Systems.

Some employees return to work not properly rested, because while they were on vacation, they were frequently contacted by workmates for basic information. However, when more employees are trained to perform the same work and have access to an Integrated Information System, then employees on vacation can be properly rested.

Everyone deserves to be properly rested when they are on vacation. Investing in machinery and Information Systems will allow an organization to have continuity even when experienced and knowledgeable employees are away.

2. Recruiting quality candidates

Another way to prevent workplace burnout is to recruit quality candidates. The cost to recruit quality candidates may be higher than recruiting ordinary persons to perform the same duties. At some interviews, leaders will consider employing candidates who request lower compensation than the others. Therefore, those leaders fail to take into consideration the certificates and experience of the candidates. There are many reasons to recruit quality candidates, and leaders must carefully consider these reasons and use them to guide future recruitment.

Figure 1. Reasons for recruiting quality candidates

Greater productivity

Reduce wastage and cost overruns

Consistent quality outputs

Lower cost for training

Linear learning curve

Enhances the organization's competiveness

Greater number of employees to become leaders

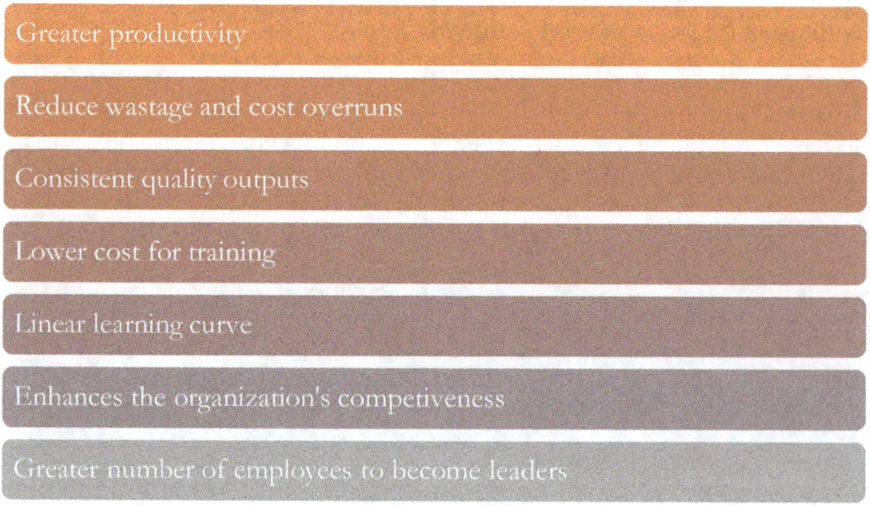

(All figures developed by the author unless otherwise noted.)

2.1 Greater productivity

When leaders are considering greater productivity, they must consider the organization's inputs. One such input is its human capital. Organizations that have been in existence for many years may already have most of the employees they need. Those who are comfortable working for that organization may not leave it anytime soon. However, if persons choose to leave that organization, then leaders must consider recruiting quality candidates to improve the organization's productivity.

Startup organizations may have a great opportunity to recruit many candidates whose certificates and experience meet the job recruitments. Although many candidates may have the same certificates, leaders must carefully give priority to those candidates who can make major impacts on the organization.

The benefits of quality employees may outweigh the extra money spent to recruit them. Leaders cannot always look at the extra dollars to be spent to acquire candidates who will help transform the organization.

2.2 Reduce wastage and cost overruns

When organizations want to reduce wastage and stop cost overruns, the recruitment of quality candidates will be one of their solutions. Organizations must have the right tools and equipment to stop cost overruns. Employees must also be trained to be effective and efficient in their work to eliminate wastage. Nevertheless, when quality candidates are recruited and are provided with the right resources, they can quickly add to the success of the organization.

2.3 Consistent quality outputs

One reason some leaders will pay more for quality candidates is that they are looking for consistent quality outputs. If an organization has many competitors, then it will be challenged to deliver consistent quality outputs, since customers have more options.

Customers sometimes become loyal to organizations because they know that they are paying for products with consistent quality. In the motor vehicle industry, for example, some customers will only purchase certain brands of vehicles because of their quality. Recruiting quality candidates is one way that leaders may be assured of consistent quality outputs.

2.4 Lower cost for training

Leaders must decide if they are willing to pay a little more for quality employees, which will result in the organization incurring lower training costs. If leaders recruit candidates whose quality is below the expected standard, then more money will have to be spent on training them to meet the organization's expectations.

Figure 2. The tradeoff between recruiting quality candidates and training costs

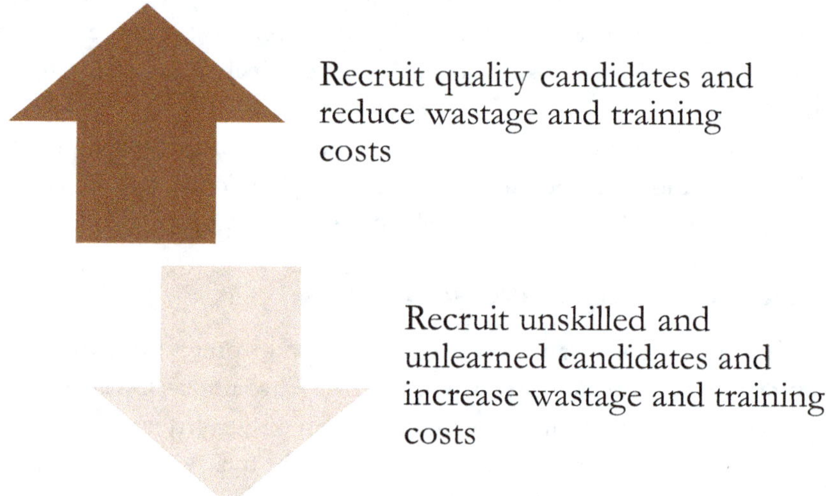

Sometimes, the money spent to increase the performance of unskilled and unlearned persons may be significant to the organization. The number of mistakes made by these employees may cause the organization to lose customers and to spend more time reworking products.

With the recruitment of quality candidates, many organizations will experience quality outputs and even an increase in production. There may be little need to incur the cost for training quality candidates, since they are already highly skilled and efficient.

When quality candidates are recruited, overtime work may be eliminated, thus preventing workplace burnout, as employees may only be required to work the standard working hours.

2.5 Linear learning curve

Within the first few days and months, employees will spend time learning about the organization and its duties. Many organizations do not have the time to wait for new employees to take months or years to become effective. Therefore, if organizations want to keep their learning curve in a straight line, they should recruit quality candidates. When quality candidates are recruited, they may quickly understand what they have to do within a short period and be able to add greater quality to the organization. Those candidates who have previous work experience may be able to join a new organization and flow easily from the very first day, especially if they were doing a similar job before.

Recruits have to be provided with much training before they are ready to occupy their substantive position and be effective. Therefore, leaders should consider recruiting quality candidates in order to keep their learning curve very low from the beginning.

2.6 Enhances the organization's competitiveness

When organizations recruit quality candidates, they give themselves opportunities to be competitive. An organization can have the best equipment and quality raw materials, but if its employees are unskilled or inexperienced, it may not meet the needs of its customers.

If an organization's outputs are outstanding, it may become the leader in the industry. Industry leaders may be able to charge a premium price for their outputs, and customers will be willing to pay that price.

2.7 Greater number of employees to become leaders

Some organizations believe in promoting those who are within the organization. These organizations will mainly advertise when they have vacancies for low-end employees.

As a result of the organization recruiting quality candidates, those employees can become great leaders. Many leaders will prefer to fill key vacancies with persons who are already in the organization, as internal recruitment will keep the organization from having to incur costs to advertise for those vacancies. Also, with internal recruitment, the employees who will be given those positions already have an understanding of the organization's culture, employees, and direction.

3. Job rotation

Managers and supervisors need their employees to do more, but they must create opportunities for employees to learn more and to practice what they have learned. Leaders must remember that they have a responsibility to properly coordinate the organization's resources so that there is continuity in the organization and employees will not become overwhelmed with their work.

Employees can become weary in doing the same thing over and over. After a while, the work becomes monotonous to them and they lose the desire to do the same thing every day. Because some employees lose their focus in doing the same work daily, they may start operating without thinking and make simple mistakes. The joy that some persons once had for their work has been lost, and they are attending work only because they need to earn.

According to Noe et al. (2015), job rotation is "The process of systematically moving a single individual from one job to another over time. The job assignments may be in various functional areas of the company, or movement may be between jobs in a single functional area or development."

In mitigating workplace burnout, some leaders may see signs in certain employees and know that they may lose interest in doing the same thing over and over again. Many employees may not complain that they have become tired of doing the same job daily, since they may think that their leaders will choose to replace them. Therefore, leaders need to assess their employees and look for signs of burnout.

3.1 Consideration for rotating employees

When an employee has been working with the same organization for many years, they often need to learn new skills. When leaders rotate their employees, they allow those employees to learn new skills.

Figure 3. Considerations for rotating employees

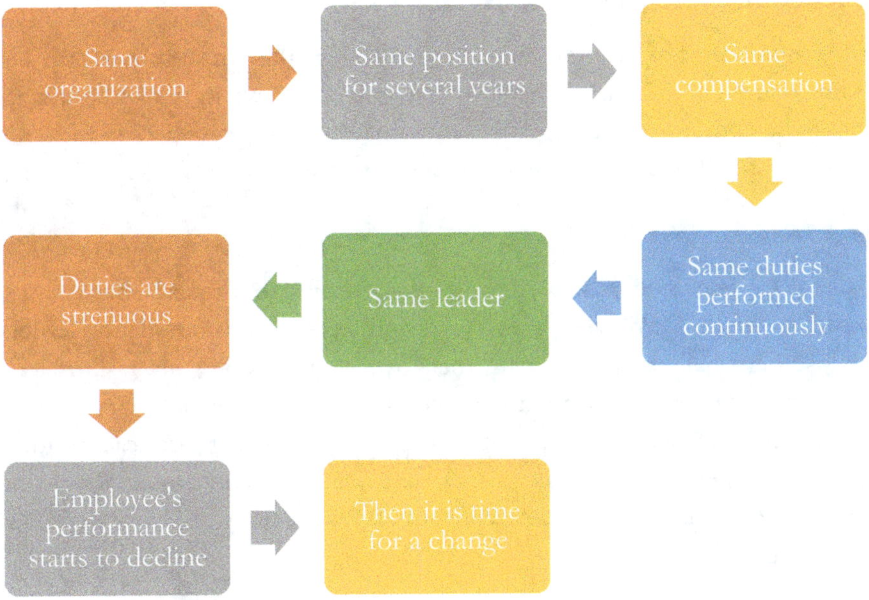

Same organization → Same position for several years → Same compensation

Same duties performed continuously → Same leader → Duties are strenuous

Employee's performance starts to decline → Then it is time for a change

3.1.1 Same organization

When employees first join organizations, they are often excited to learn new things. However, when they have been in the same organization for many years, they sometimes lose their interest in it, especially if there are no signs of progress in the organization.

3.1.2 Same position for several years

Being in the same position for many years can be disturbing. In some organizations, employees may remain in the same position for many years, despite new employees being recruited and the long-standing employees having to train the new employees.

3.1.3 Same compensation

Most employees expect increases in compensation, probably annually or at least within three years. However, some employees work for the same organization for years while receiving the same compensation, despite how much work they do for the organization.

3.1.4 Same duties performed continuously

Employees can become mentally tired when they have to perform the same duties continuously. They sometimes do not have to think about what has to be done, since their bodies are automatically programed to do the same thing over and over again. They may be doing these duties for several years.

3.1.5 Same leader

For some persons, the work may be interesting, but their leaders do not motivate them. Employees often try to find ways of accommodating leaders whose personalities conflict with their own. Some leaders are taskmasters, and there are others who are narcissists. With these leadership types, employees can become weary of having to work with those leaders for a prolonged period, since the leaders are not too concerned about the employees' well-being but more concerned about getting the work done and receiving praise.

3.1.6 Duties are strenuous

The tasks that some employees do are very mild, and they find joy in performing those duties. However, some employees do much more strenuous work that may require much thinking even when they are not at work. For example, attending to customers' complaints can be challenging, since many customers will express their frustration for even the smallest of things. When some customers are having personal issues, they may not be able to separate their issues from other things that are troubling them, so when they communicate with the organization's customer representatives, they vent their personal issues at the representatives.

Some work may be strenuous on the body. For example, some employees may be required to fetch heavy materials, especially in organizations where much of the work is done manually.

3.1.7 Employee's performance starts to decline

After a while, with all of the challenges some employees go through, their work performance will decline. Sometimes, even the best of employees may show signs of decline in their work because their work is too repetitive.

3.1.8 Then it is time for a change

When leaders recognize that employees are becoming tired of doing the same thing and their performance is declining, it may be a good sign to rotate them. Leaders should not wait until employees become frustrated with the organization before rotating them. When employees grow tired of the organization, they may start looking for other employment opportunities to keep their interest in work alive.

3.2 Strategic plan to rotate employees

Rotating employees must become part of the organization's Strategic Human Resources plan. This will require management to have a deliberate intention to rotate employees, thus giving them opportunities to perform new and different functions within the organization.

3.3 Greater efficiency

Rotating employees is important for leaders to do because it enables employees to become more efficient within the organization. While some employees may lose interest in the tasks they are performing, once they are rotated, they may find renewed energy to continue working with the organization and giving their best effort.

Some leaders believe that employees who have been performing a specific task for a long duration may be efficient. That may be true. However, when something new is given to the same employee, they may demonstrate greater efficiency, as they are doing something that challenges them to complete.

Employees who have recently been assigned to new tasks may want to outshine those who were doing the same tasks before them. In so doing, the new appointees to those positions may be looking for opportunities to work permanently in those departments or to perform those functions in the future.

Organizations sometimes benefit greatly from job rotations. Employees who are assigned to new positions may now find themselves doing jobs they have always wanted to do.

3.4 Multi-skilled employees

When leaders rotate employees, they enable those employees to become multi-skilled, which will cause organizations to have multiple employees who can perform the same job. Many times, when only one employee can perform a particular job, that person can use their influence and power to hold the organization at ransom. However, when many employees can perform the same job, the organization will continue its normal operation even if some of those experienced employees choose to leave.

Job rotation is necessary for most organizations. However, leaders must plan to make job rotation an effective task. There are times when persons are rotated, but the organization does not benefit greatly from them.

Figure 4. Making job rotation effective

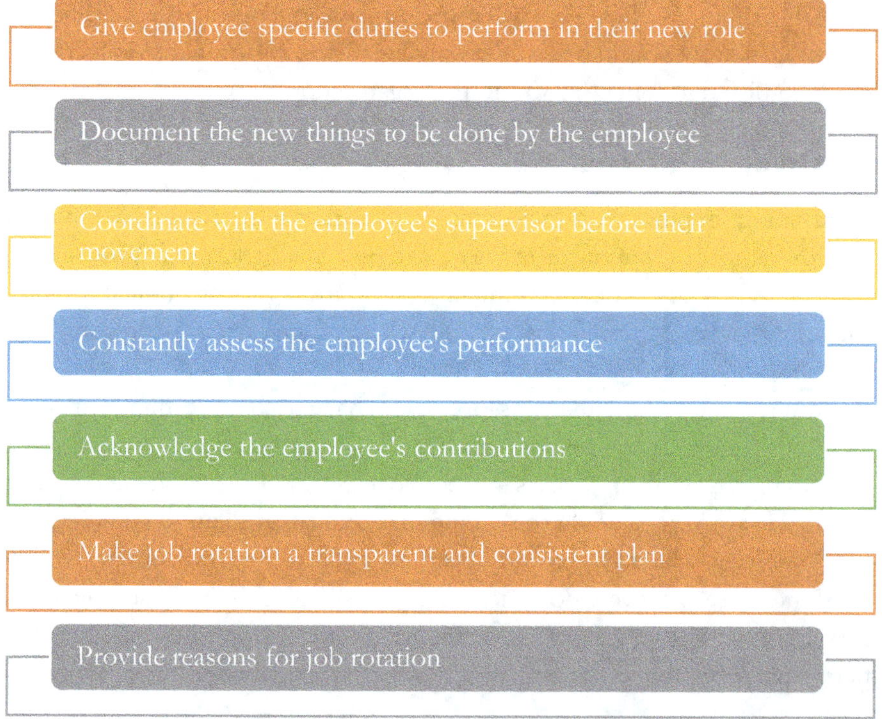

3.4.1 Give employee specific duties to perform in their new role

When rotating an employee, it is important to give that employee specific duties to perform. It is unacceptable to send an employee to a new department or a desk without assigning them specific tasks.

Some organizations may recruit some persons to be management trainees. These recruits will have the opportunity to move from one department to another to enhance their knowledge of the organization's activities. Therefore, when the management trainees are assigned to a designation, they will operate effectively. Whenever management trainees are assigned to different departments, they must be given specific duties to perform.

3.4.2 Document the new things to be done by the employee

Having duties written down is a good way to avoid conflicts. Employees who are rotated must be given specific duties to perform. Before they leave their current position to occupy a temporary position, they must know in advance what they are required to do. Many times, it is preferred to provide employees with the temporary duties in writing, so that they can always refer to that written document. For those employees who have to work in the factory, field, or some outdoor activities, they may be informed verbally of their new duties.

3.4.3 Coordinate with the employee's supervisor before their movement

If a manager has arranged the job rotation, then the supervisors must be informed of the employee's movement. Even if the owner of the organization wants to rotate the employee, at least the employee's supervisor must be informed in advance of the move. Sometimes, it is important to inform all staff within the department or section about the rotation of employees so that there will not be confusion in the department.

When employees perform duties in a department and have to be rotated, their sudden absence may create unease or suspicion among the other employees. However, if the employees are informed of the reason when a coworker is rotated to another department or desk, then they may feel more comfortable and support management for future decision-making.

3.4.4 Constantly assess the employee's performance

Those employees who are on rotation must have their performance assessed. When employees know that their performance is being assessed, they will constantly want to do everything necessary to prove that they are quality employees. Once employees have specific duties, then it becomes easy to assess their performance.

3.4.5 Acknowledge the employee's contributions

Managers and supervisors must acknowledge employees' performance. Sometimes, however little acknowledgment may be shown, it may motivate employees to improve their performance. Employees who are on rotation like to know what their leaders think of their performance. If their performance needs improvement, then it must be brought to their attention very early so that they can improve whatever they have to do.

3.4.6 Make job rotation a transparent and consistent plan

If job rotation is done in secret, then it may raise suspicion among employees. Every employee wants to know that they are eligible for job rotation so that they can enhance their skills. When job rotation is transparent, management may get the best performance from their employees.

Job rotation must also be consistent. If the leaders agreed to rotate employees every year, then that must be done. The employees who are selected to be rotated must meet whatever criteria were established. Long-serving employees may be distracted if they see persons who have recently been hired being provided with opportunities to be rotated before them.

3.4.7 Provide reasons for job rotation

Leaders should provide reasons why they are rotating particular employees. If the organization plans to rotate its employees regularly, then it may be important for the Human Resources policies to include information about job rotation. This information must be clear so that all employees know why other employees will be rotated and understand the benefits of job rotation. Leaders must be willing to place their thinking into written documents so that employees will know the requirements for job rotation.

4. Training and developing employees

Leaders must be willing to invest in the lives of their employees. This will be done through training and development.

Some employees are willing to take on new challenges, but they are fearful since they do not know those new positions. However, with some amount of training, those fears may disappear, and those employees may be willing to occupy new positions or be transferred to another department.

Training is a planned effort to facilitate the learning of job-related knowledge, skills, and behaviour by employees. (Noe et al., 2015)

4.1 Internal training for employees

Leaders may think that the training that their employees need must be provided externally. There will always be advantages and disadvantages of external training. Sometimes, the training that employees need can be provided from within the organization.

Figure 5. Benefits of internal training for employees

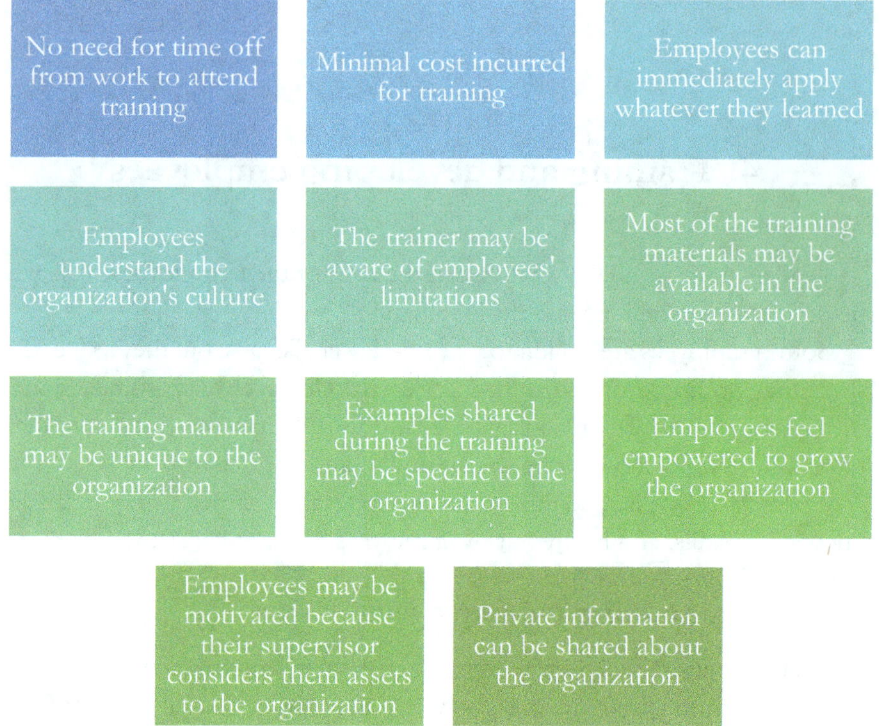

4.1.1 No need for time off from work to attend training

When external training is away from the office, the supervisor will have to provide time off to the employee, including time to travel to and from the training location. If employees have to travel long distances for external training, then the organization will lose productive hours from the employees. However, for internal training, no time off is needed, since the employees are within the same section, building, or organization.

4.1.2 Minimal cost incurred for training

Most times, for internal training, the organization does not have to provide transport or traveling allowance in order for employees to attend. For some external training, organizations may have to incur meal allowance for their employees. However, meal allowance may not be applicable for internal training, since employees will continue their usual arrangement of providing for their meals.

4.1.3 Employees can immediately apply whatever they learned

If employees are trained externally, some of the information they receive may not be applicable to their organization. However, with internal training, employees will be able to apply what they learn within the organization. Sometimes, as part of the employee's training, they may be provided with access to the machine, equipment, etc., soon after receiving the training. Therefore, they will be able to apply their knowledge at the earliest possible moment after they are trained.

4.1.4 Employees understand the organization's culture

Not knowing the culture of an organization can be a barrier to training. However, internal training eliminates that barrier. Because employees may be trained by another employee of the same organization, they both will understand the organization's culture. When training is provided by external trainers, the trainers may not know the culture of the organization, and therefore, they may not be able to refer to specific cultural issues during their training. Without saying much, internal trainers may convey the organizational culture, and the trainees may embrace that culture quickly.

4.1.5 The trainer may be aware of employees' limitations

Each employee has their limitations, no matter how great they are perceived to be. Sometimes, the trainer may be provided with updates on the employee's limitations, so the training may be specific to help those employees to overcome their limitations. For example, customer service training may be provided to some employees by a manager from the Marketing or Human Capital department. The trainer may address the employees' shortcomings and may involve the trainees in role-playing with other employees with whom they are already familiar.

Some managers are very good at working in the factory and field, but may not be good at administrative functions. Therefore, they will be provided with training in completing reports and learning how to interact with employees, especially if those are some of their weak areas.

4.1.6 Most of the training materials may be available in the organization

Many trainers will try to provide materials when training employees. When training is done internally, many of the materials needed may already be available within the organization, so the trainer does not have to gather other materials.

For example, if recruits have to be trained about an organization's Mission, Vision, Goals, Objectives, Key Performance Indicators, and Critical Success Factors, then information will already be available for this training. Some managers may need to be trained on how to prepare a department budget. The trainer may be able to retrieve the previous year's budget and use it as the training material for the current period.

Training about Health and Safety is important for all employees to know. The organization may have a Health and Safety policy, procedure, or other documents that will be used for this specific training.

4.1.7 The training manual may be unique to the organization

If training is provided regularly, then the organization may have some specific manuals. These manuals will be updated periodically and be used to train employees. For example, some organizations may have an orientation manual for new employees. Many departments have a desk manual or Standard Operating Procedures (SOP) that can be used as training material.

4.1.8 Examples shared during the training may be specific to the organization

Trainers will sometimes ask trainees to share examples. When this happens, employees can share examples that are specific to the organization, and most of the trainees may understand those examples. When internal examples are used, it may resonate more with the trainees.

4.1.9 Employees feel empowered to grow the organization

With the training they receive, employees will feel a sense of personal satisfaction to help grow the organization. The training may provide examples of how trainees can apply the information within the organization. For example, training may be provided to sales agents, and specific examples may include how sales agents can help the organization to increase sales.

If employees know that the organization is not experiencing good financial health, they may try to increase sales or reduce costs, since their compensation depends upon the success of the organization. Trainees may receive training on how to identify wastage and cost overruns in the organization and how they can reduce or eliminate those unnecessary costs.

Figure 6. Employees that are trained can enhance the organization's profit

4.1.10 Employees may be motivated because their supervisor considers them assets to the organization

Employees sometimes feel that they are not valuable to the organization. However, when their supervisor selects them for training, they may be motivated and feel a sense of appreciation that someone has considered them an asset to the organization. Because internal training may have a minimal cost, more persons may be chosen to attend the training.

4.1.11 Private information can be shared about the organization

During training, there may be the need to share some private information. For example, the organization's financial performance may be discussed, especially if the training intends to help employees to grow the organization's profit. If the organization's Mission Statement has to be reviewed, then some private information may be shared about why the current Mission Statement may not apply to the future direction of the organization.

When external trainers are providing examples during the training, they generally have to avoid mentioning confidential information which they may know about other organizations. However, an internal trainer can use many internal examples, since all information is expected to remain confidential among the trainees. For example, if there have been breaches of internal controls that led to pilfering, those examples can be used.

4.2 External training for employees

An organization may not always be able to provide internal training to its employees. Every supervisor and manager must determine if they have the internal resources to provide training, and if the answer is no, then they must consider external training.

Figure 7. Benefits of external training for employees

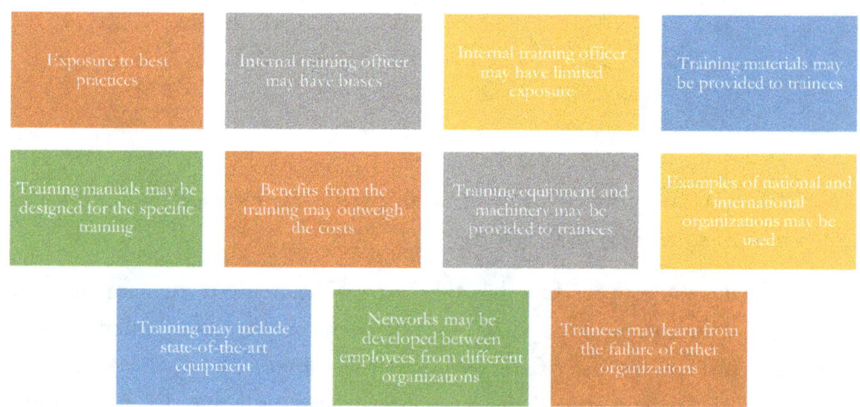

4.2.1 Exposure to best practices

The external representatives who are responsible for training may be able to provide information about best practices. They might have dealt with many different scenarios and know what is happening in different industries or in other countries.

External trainers may be the developers of some of the things that employees need to know. Sometimes, lecturers, professionals, and retirees may be used to provide external training because of the wide exposure of knowledge and experience.

4.2.2 Internal training officers may have biases

Internal trainers may be biased in their views and express those biases in the training. If the organization is performing well, they may operate as though their organization is the best. On the other hand, if the organization's performance is poor, some trainers may talk about the negative aspects of the organization, which may demotivate the trainees.

4.2.3 Internal training officers may have limited exposure

Although some internal training officers may have received formal education for specific learning, they may be limited in their knowledge and exposure. When training is provided, many trainees will welcome the opportunity to have a wide expanse of knowledge and exposure shared with them.

Some internal trainers may have limited working experience, or they may have worked very long with the same organization and not be familiar with recent developments in a particular subject area.

4.2.4 Training materials may be provided to the trainees

Internal training officers may not provide any training material along with the training, since they believe that employees understand the organization and the things that happen within it. Not all internal training officers may take the time to provide written information for the training, since they may mainly share from their own experience.

However, many external trainers will provide some amount of training materials. Sometimes, if these materials are not provided during the training session, a soft copy may be emailed to the trainees or be sent to the Human Capital Department for onward distribution to the trainees.

Many times, because the external training has a cost attached to it, the trainer will attempt to provide whatever training materials they can.

4.2.5 Training manuals may be designed for the specific training

If external trainers are providing the same training consistently, they may design training manuals, which will make their training consistent. The external trainer may also take time to modify their training manuals with additional information. That may be relevant since they want to provide fresh and up-to-date information to their trainees, and they probably want to stand out against other persons who are providing the same training.

4.2.6 Benefits from the training may outweigh the costs

Employees who were sent on external training sometimes return to the organization and praise their supervisor for sending them on the training, because they are rejuvenated. The leaders may recognize that the benefits received by the employees outweigh the cost of the training. If the leaders have sent previous batches of employees to the same external training, they may have seen the transforming impact of the training on the employees.

4.2.7 Training equipment and machinery may be provided to trainees

Not all organizations may have the equipment and the right types of machinery needed for the training. Therefore, leaders may send employees on training courses to organizations and learning institutions that have the machinery to equip the trainees. The cost to invest in the required equipment and machinery may be outside of the reach of some organizations, so they may establish a Memorandum of Understanding (MOU) with another organization or person to provide training to their employees.

4.2.8 Examples of national and international organizations may be used

When training is provided by external trainers, they may include examples of national and international organizations. These external trainers might have worked in international organizations and have first-hand information to share with the trainees. Sometimes, the external training may be done overseas and the trainees may be exposed to international information.

4.2.9 Training may include state-of-the-art equipment

The training provided may include information about the state-of-the-art equipment and machinery. Not every organization may have the finances to regularly update or change their machinery and equipment, but with external training, they may receive such information.

4.2.10 Networks may be developed between employees from different organizations

Employees who are sent on external training may meet employees from other organizations who are doing the same course. During the training, networking may be established, which will allow employees from the various organizations to share their failures and successes. In cases where one employee is very proficient in a particular area, that experience can be shared with another employee who needs one-on-one training.

4.2.11 Trainees may learn from the failure of other organizations

From external training, trainees may learn about the failures of other organizations. There are times when employees feel that their organization is the worst, only to learn that there are other organizations that are experiencing even more challenges.

4.3 What to expect in a training plan

When leaders are developing a training plan to manage their employees and to prevent workplace burnout, they must include certain important things in their plan. If an organization conducts regular training, then they may have many of these things already.

Figure 8. Training plan will include

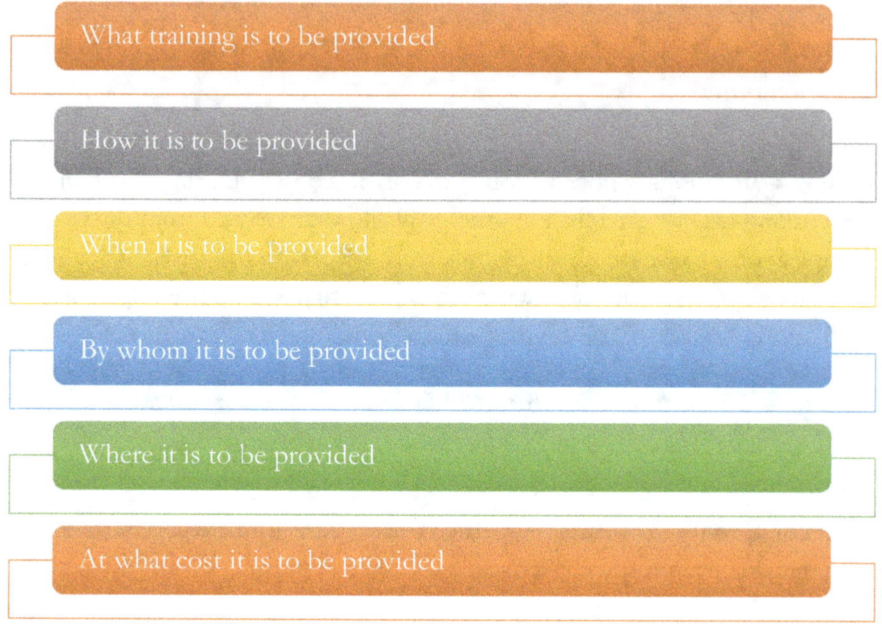

(Extract from Cole, 1993)

Some organizations may have a specific department that provides training. Such a department may be referred to as the "Training Department," and it may be independent of the Human Capital Department. Other organizations will have an independent unit within the Human Capital Department that is assigned to identify the training needs of employees and to facilitate those needs. In the event training cannot be facilitated from internal resources, then external resources will be sought to equip employees.

When more employees are properly trained and given opportunities to rotate within the organization, then the leaders have more employees who can be moved around within the organization, thus preventing any one employee from becoming overworked and frustrated.

4.4 Keeping training costs low

Many times, leaders see training costs as a great expense to the organization. However, the cost to replace an employee may be more than the cost to train them. When employees are burnt out, they may suddenly resign, since they believe that their employer does not care about their health.

Some employees have been performing the same task for many years and need a change. Therefore, they expect that their leaders will provide them with some amount of training and reassign them to different departments or duties.

While training costs can be expensive for some organizations, leaders must look for ways of keeping those costs as minimal as possible without compromising the quality of the training. When employees see that their leaders consider them for training and invest money in their training, they often want to make greater contributions to an organization that cares for them. A little investment in an employee today may prevent workplace burnout and cause an organization to have great success in the future.

The illustration below shows some ways to reduce training costs. Leaders must provide training to their employees and see the organization grow.

Figure 9. Ways to reduce training costs

- Train many employees at once
- Document processes or procedures of how tasks are to be completed
- Establish manuals for tasks
- Engage each person within each department to train at least one person in that department
- Job rotation
- Upload recent training video, manual, etc., on intranet, website, social media
- Recruit highly skilled and experienced staff who are within the same industry or have operated in the same position

4.5 Development for employees

Leaders must have a plan for the development of their human capital. Every employee is an important asset to the organization, but they need the support of their leaders if the organization is to become successful. It is the leaders' responsibility to be strategic in their thinking and establish an employee developmental plan, which is expected to give them a pool of human resources that they can draw from whenever the need arises.

To prevent workplace burnout, before an employee becomes tired, leaders can organize for employees to utilize their vacation and for other employees to fill the void. Leaders must also develop employees to become leaders. Too often, when senior employees leave the organization, there is a sudden rush to find a replacement. However, if the leaders have spent time developing other employees, then there should be internal persons who can fill those voids within the shortest possible time.

Leaders must have a plan for how and when they will develop particular employees. While all employees cannot be developed at the same time, some employees must be identified and be given opportunities for development. With an increasing number of employees who are ready to help the organization to grow and provide continued support, then there is a greater possibility of preventing workplace burnout and more leaders to take the organization in the same direction.

Figure 10. Approaches to employee development

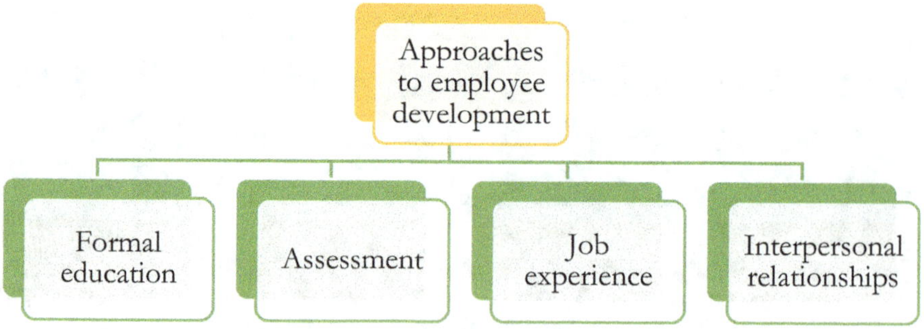

(Developed from Noe et al., 2015)

Some organizations may have policies where they will allocate a certain percentage or number of employees who can attend development courses within a given time. With this policy, some employees will be developed, which can lead towards their upward movement within the organization. Other employees will then be considered for the next training session or be rotated so that they are better equipped for the success of the organization.

Developing employees can be done through on-the-job sessions as well as sessions away from the organization. Not all of the development that an employee needs will be provided through formal approaches.

Leaders must be willing to assess their employees and determine what can be done to develop them. Leaders may have to allocate money in their departmental budget for employee development, but the benefits will be great. Employees like to know that their leaders care about them and are willing to give them opportunities to grow.

Developing more junior employees can prevent many leaders from becoming burnt out. Some leaders may experience fatigue and begin to make many mistakes. This may be a sign that they need to rest, and it may also act as a trigger to remind them that they must develop other employees to become leaders so that they can proceed on vacation and prevent workplace burnout.

5. Succession planning

No leader will remain with an organization forever. Some leaders believe that if they are not at work, the organization cannot function effectively in their absence. However, the owner of the organization must prevent any of their employees from holding the organization to ransom.

According to Noe et al. (2015), succession planning includes "The identification and tracking of high-potential employees capable of filling higher-level managerial positions."

5.1 Identify the need for more leaders

Leaders must identify if there is an urgent need to develop more leaders. This is important, because if some employees have recently been trained to become new leaders, then a need may not exist immediately.

5.2 Identify employees with potential leadership abilities

Once the need exists for more leaders, efforts must be made to identify potential leaders. If many employees show signs of leadership abilities, then there will be a need to determine which set of employees will be trained now and who will be trained at a later time.

Within some organizations, there may be many employees with the necessary experience and academic requirements to become new leaders. However, the organization may have a quota of employees who can be trained to become new leaders immediately.

Whenever leaders identify potential new leaders, they must communicate to those employees that management has an interest in them and wants to provide them with opportunities to become future leaders. If potential leaders are not aware that management is interested in them, they may lose hope in the organization and begin searching for new employment opportunities.

5.3 Invest in them

Once new leaders are identified, then it is time to invest in them. There must not be any fear in investing in potential leaders, since they may be able to transform the organization. Some organizations have gone through a crisis where some of the leaders suddenly leave and the existing employees are not aware of how to continue the organization's activities.

Leaders may leave an organization for many reasons. Their exit from the organization must not cause panic, since new leaders have been identified and trained.

Figure 11. Possible reasons leaders may not remain with the organization indefinitely

5.4 Give them opportunities to function

Potential leaders must be given opportunities to function in the position they are likely to assume. The developmental session in the organization must allow these potential leaders to have the opportunity to operate as though they were already in that position. If the substantive leaders proceed on vacation, the potential leaders must be placed to act in that capacity until the substantial leaders return to work.

When new leaders are identified and given opportunities to function in those capacities, it can prevent the existing leaders from being burnt out. Many leaders often work long hours because they do not have anyone understudying them.

5.5 Reward them in the future

One of the reasons some employees do not want to take up leadership positions is that they work very hard but are hardly compensated. Some trainees may hear from their leaders that they will only be rewarded when they occupy a substantial position. However, established leaders should consider compensating their trainees now or in the near future. Whatever little reward may be offered, it may motivate some trainees.

While many trainees know that they are on training and may not be entitled to full compensation, they must be aware that they will receive some portion of compensation. Many potential leaders are motivated by whatever compensation is offered to them.

6. Vacation options

When organizations are designing their Human Capital policies, they must include different types of vacations. Most organizations that have been in existence for many years will already have vacation policies.

Providing employees with vacation is very important for all employers to do. While employees are there to help organizations deliver their products and services, every employee deserves some vacation.

6.1 Sufficient vacation for employees

When leaders are determining the number of vacation days to be provided to employees, they must take into consideration the challenges of certain jobs. This will be important to prevent workplace burnout. With some jobs, employees must have more time away from work so that they can be rested and return to the organization energized.

6.2 Annual vacation

Many organizations provide their employees with annual vacations. While on vacation, the employees will be paid for their time away from the organization.

In some organizations, employees are only allowed to proceed on their first annual vacation after they have completed their first year of service. Some organizations are flexible and will prorate employees' annual vacation so that they can utilize the portion of their vacation that they have earned. Therefore, if employees are entitled to four weeks' vacation, then if they have completed six months of work, they may be entitled to a two-week vacation. If those employees wait until the end of their first year, then they can utilize their full four weeks' vacation all at once.

6.3 Compassionate vacation

Organizations may provide a compassionate vacation to employees who have lost a loved one or close family member. Each organization will establish requirements for employees to proceed on compassionate vacation.

6.4 Certified sick leave

Occasionally, employees will become ill and need to be away from the organization, and they may be entitled to certified sick leave. To apply for this leave, they will have to produce medical documents to show that they visited a professional medical practitioner and received some medical time away from the organization.

6.5 Uncertified sick leave

Some organizations may have a specific amount of uncertified sick leave to which employees are entitled. Therefore, these employees can report sick without producing a medical certificate. For example, employees may be feeling unwell and report ill for that day.

6.6 Examination leave

Employees should be encouraged to increase their academics. When they are ready to write their examinations, then they can apply for their examination leave, and they may be paid while they are away from the organization. Many organizations like to know that they have employees who are willing to increase their knowledge. When more employees increase their knowledge, they provide themselves with great opportunities to be promoted and add great value to the organization.

7. Scheduling of work

Leaders have a responsibility to schedule their subordinates' work. There are times when certain tasks can be very stringent. Therefore, leaders can have several persons involved in completing those tasks or select employees who can complete the work in the shortest possible time, with great accuracy, especially if there is a sudden demand to complete the work.

7.1 Minimizing overtime

Overtime work must not be a normal thing; it should only be applied when the work demand is outside of the norm. Some employees are burnt out because they have to perform their routine duties and are still required to work extra hours regularly to meet the organization's demands.

There are several ways to reduce overtime and prevent workplace burnout. This will involve the leaders employing more persons to complete the same work. There is another option available to management, which involves the use of modern technology and machinery.

7.2 Shift system

Having a shift system is another way of allowing the same amount of work to be completed without causing employees to be burnt out. For example, some employees may work the first eight hours, and another shift will continue for the following eight hours. Therefore, whatever work was left incomplete by the previous shift will be completed by the next shift.

Consider the rehabilitation of a major road. There may be one team that works for eight hours, and then the other team will take over, since the work has to be completed within the shortest possible time. When some tasks are demanding and have a great impact on customers, then the leaders must carefully allocate the work into the shift system, if possible. With the shift system, the same amount of work will be done, but by different employees at different times.

7.3 Rotating employees

Another way of scheduling work is to rotate employees. This will disrupt the way some employees think and operate. However, leaders must prevent workplace burnout and rotate their employees so that the same amount of work is completed. For example, one team may complete a task this week, and another team may be given the same responsibility for the following week. Therefore, with that arrangement, no team is completely assigned on a full-time basis to complete particular tasks.

In the planting and harvesting of crops, some of the employees may work in the field one week, and then the next week, they will work on processing the crops that are harvested. When these employees are rotated to work in the factory, the fieldwork will be completed by those who were in the factory the previous week.

7.4 Recruit more persons to complete difficult work

Leaders think about the number of persons they have to hire and think that they would have to spend too much money. However, when the work is strenuous, it may be a good option to employ more persons to complete the same task. For example, because some work is seasonal, there may be the option of increasing the labor force whenever there is a high demand for that work. Once the demand has reduced, those temporary employees will no longer be needed.

During the last quarter of the calendar year, some organizations may experience an increase in sales. Therefore, temporary persons may be employed to address the peak season, and after the peak season is over, the labor force will be back to normal. This approach is taken to prevent workplace burnout and to allow the organization to meet customer demand.

Sometimes, when there is a backlog of work, more persons may be employed. These temporary employees will only be assigned to reduce the backlog and to bring the organization's workload to a manageable level.

8. Monitoring work regularly

Leaders must monitor their employees' work regularly. With regular monitoring, leaders will know the volume of work that has to be completed and what may be outstanding.

8.1 Reports of work completed

Leaders should have a system in place where they can receive updates from their employees concerning the work they have completed. There must be regular feedback from employees about completed tasks, whether formal or informal.

Leaders must determine if they need daily, weekly or monthly reports of work completed. This information must be communicated so that each employee team will submit their reports according to the timeframe assigned to them.

8.2 Reports of outstanding work

Some leaders need to know what the outstanding tasks are. Based upon this information, they will determine the workforce they need to complete this work.

In cases where the leaders are directly involved with the employees, a formal report may not be necessary, since the leader knows what was completed. Some leaders are in the same department or on the construction site with their team, so they know exactly what was completed within a specific timeframe. Some employees enjoy when their leaders are there with them, since if something unusual happens, there will be a quick response from the leader as to the best possible option for addressing the matter.

8.3 Regular inspection by the leaders

Leaders must inspect the work completed by their subordinates. For example, when employees operate in the office, they will submit some of their written documents to their supervisors to be checked off. This approach allows the supervisors to know how the employee is progressing and to correct anything that may be wrong at the time of inspection.

If employees have to work in the factory, field, etc., then the leaders must check with them at the worksite to see how they have progressed with their work. Leaders must be willing to be around their subordinates in order to see how the work is progressing and offer any advice if the need arises.

Some leaders do not want to visit the worksite but constantly wait for reports to be submitted to them. Indeed, some leaders may be very busy, but they must take some time to see and know what is happening with their employees. When employees know that their leaders will inspect their work, they may work more diligently to complete their work on time and at an acceptable level.

Regular monitoring of work by leaders lets them know if their subordinates are managing their task very well or if some employees are showing signs of tiredness or fatigue. Some leaders may be observant to prevent workplace burnout as they regularly monitor the work of their employees.

9. Establishing and enforcing review systems

Employees are not always burnt out from doing the correct things; it may be because they have to spend time correcting errors made by them, by other employees, or by the system. Leaders may want to cut costs, but they must think of a systematic way of reducing costs while still allowing the organization to meet the needs of the customers.

9.1 Quality products at the beginning

Sometimes, too much cost is incurred in reviewing products and services received. If an organization arranges to do business with companies and persons whose products and services are reputable, it can reduce the time needed to review those items.

Many organizations are working towards becoming International Organization for Standardization (ISO) certified. When organizations are ISO certified, other organizations may engage them to deliver products and services which may minimize or altogether eliminate the inspection stage. Organizations that are ISO certified are expected to maintain their standard since they can lose their certification if they do not.

Every time an employee has to stop what they are doing to review a product, it may slow down the operation. When quality products are purchased, they can go straight into production without any review.

9.2 Identify a person for review

When an organization has established a system of review, it will have to assign a person to review the products and services received. When a person is assigned to this task, then other employees can concentrate on their main duties.

9.3 Establish a system for review

Many organizations have established internal controls, some of which may include regular reviews. The frequency of reviews may be indicated. Organizations whose products and services meet the organization's expectations will not require much review, if any. However, those organizations whose performance is not always consistent may require regular reviews.

9.4 Reviewing the inputs

Before putting products into production, it is important to review them in order to detect any problems. With early detection of problems, those products will not be included in the production process, thus reducing the need for employees to spend extra time correcting the outputs.

When more time and money are spent reviewing inputs, the organization can also reduce overtime and the other production costs associated with overtime work. Employees can become overwhelmed in repeating the same process over and over because the input had faults that were not detected before production commenced.

10. Upgrading of workplace equipment

Leaders must show their willingness to prevent workplace burnout by upgrading workplace equipment. All machinery will have its lifespan. Once that lifespan has expired, it is time to upgrade the equipment.

10.1 Regular maintenance of equipment

Equipment requires regular maintenance, even new equipment. It is amazing how two organizations may have the same equipment, from the same manufacturer, purchased at the same time, but with differences in performance. Sometimes, the difference in performance is based upon how frequently the equipment was serviced. Just like the human body, equipment needs regular medical checkups and time for rest.

Manufacturers may also indicate the number of hours that the equipment can work before it is time for maintenance. If employers respect and follow that guidance, they may get more done with the equipment they have purchased. Regular and timely maintenance may prevent the breakdown of equipment.

10.2 Establishing service logs for equipment

Both leaders and subordinates should establish service logs for the equipment. These logs will indicate much useful information to leaders, which will guide their decision-making. It is important to update the service logs every time work is completed and to mention if there are any defects.

Leaders may be aware if employees are not utilizing the equipment properly, since the service log will provide that useful information. For example, vehicles that were recently purchased may have to be taken frequently to the mechanic shop for service, while vehicles that were purchased earlier are still working in good order. Sometimes, when people do not get the equipment to do what they want, they blame the equipment rather than their lack of knowledge on its effective use.

10.3 Upgrading and replacing equipment

After regular maintenance, it may be time to upgrade or replace some of the equipment. If leaders continue to keep equipment that has outperformed its useful life, it may start to malfunction. With regular malfunctioning and breakdowns of equipment, employees can become frustrated. This frustration may cause employees to be exhausted and soon, their performance may diminish. Leaders have a responsibility to upgrade and replace equipment on time to prevent workplace burnout.

11. Outsourcing non-core activities

To prevent workplace burnout, leaders can outsource some non-core activities. This is a key approach, since it frees the leaders from the time needed to perform activities that will not add significant benefits to the organization.

"Outsourcing refers to organizations buying in service and expertise rather than employing their staff to perform the function" (ACCA 2.1, 2001).

11.1 Identify what can be best done by external resources

Every leader must assess their business operation and see which activities can be best performed within the organization. Some leaders think that whatever activities their organization started from its inception must continue within the organization. But times have changed, and sometimes the activities that employees were once engaged in may be better performed by external persons and organizations.

However, leaders must be mindful not to outsource activities for which they have the resources to compete. Some activities may be retained within the organization, and employees must know that they have to constantly do their best to help their organization to be successful. Some organizations may choose to maintain their own payroll and Human Capital department, since there may be personal and complex information about employees that they do not want other persons and organizations to access.

11.2 Identify what can be best done by external resources

These are some activities of operation that can more easily be outsourced. However, leaders must carefully assess these activities, and once they are confident that these activities can be outsourced, they can proceed with the relevant arrangements. These are some services that organizations may outsource so that they can spend more time concentrating on critical matters for the organization:

- Janitorial service
- Transporting employees to and from work
- Recruitment and selection of candidates for employment
- Transporting raw materials to the organization
- Repairs and maintenance of vehicles
- Repairs and maintenance of the building
- Servicing of office equipment and computers
- Security services

11.3 Consider time and cost when outsourcing

Before leaders agree to outsource certain services, they must consider the cost of doing so and conduct a cost-benefit analysis. While many leaders consider the financial impact on the organization, they must also consider the social impact that outsourcing can have on their employees.

When activities are outsourced, leaders must form arrangements with the external firm to be able to deliver the product or service on time. Some external firms may be operating some distance away from the organization that needs their assistance. With this in mind, organizations that have to outsource some products and services may want to award contracts to firms that are within a shorter distance to respond to their request.

If supplying firms are a long distance away, it can hinder the smooth flow of the organization. The supplying firm may be required to have their staff work in a shift system to meet the needs of their clients who will request their services regularly.

11.4 Establish SLA

Whenever outsourcing becomes necessary, both entities may be required to have a formal arrangement, which is often done through a Service Level Agreement (SLA). With the SLA, both entities will clearly state the terms and conditions to which they will agree. They will also establish the pricing for the goods or services.

After the SLA is established, both entities are expected to proceed and do business with each other, where one entity will be the provider and the other will be the receiver. Most times, each SLA will be established for a specific duration.

The user of the service or product is expected to assess the performance of the service provided. Just because the service provider has signed the SLA, that does not mean that they will always deliver according to expectations. During the assessment of the service provider's performance, if the user is not in agreement with the service or product provided, that information must be conveyed to the service provider at the earliest moment so that correction can be made, or a refund can be offered.

Some service providers deliver quality service at the initial stage, but as time goes by, their service diminishes. The procuring entity must hold the service provider accountable at all times for quality service to be delivered. The user must also ensure that they do the correct things and also make payment on time to the service provider.

12. Use of Information Systems and Technology

Most employees are smart and can work hard, but there are times when they need the support of machinery to make their work easier. Employees may be burnt out because most of the work that they have to do is done manually. Therefore, leaders ought to consider acquiring and using Information Technology and Information Systems within the organization.

For example, some organizations have invested in Human Resources software, which assists in selecting applications that meet the organization's requirements. With such software, most organizations can eliminate some of the manual work that is done within the Human Capital Department.

Some software is interconnected with the Inventory module and will be able to generate Purchase Request (PR) and Purchase Order (PO) based upon the inventory levels. With the use of this software, leaders can expect consistent reports, and there is no excuse from an employee about forgetting to prepare these documents.

Humans will make mistakes from time to time, even those who are experienced and knowledgeable. However, with the use of software, the organization can expect to have consistent performance and great accuracy.

12.1 Eliminate manual work

The use of Information Technology and Information Systems provides employers with the option to eliminate many tasks. Some organizations spend too much time with employees to perform functions that can be easily be completed by machinery. Organizations may need to make some investments in Information Technology, but the benefits will be great.

Several years ago, employees entered their attendance in a time book. However, with the use of a biometric attendance machine, employees will press their fingers on the machine and departmental leaders will know what time the employees arrive and leave each day. The information from this machine may be linked to the payroll, so employees who have come to work after the required time may have deductions from their wages due to late attendance.

In cases where employees work overtime, the machine will provide the number of overtime hours. Once the overtime hours are approved, those hours will be provided to the Human Capital Department and will be included in the payroll.

Many years ago, when items were sold in stores, employees would update bin cards with the items sold. However, with the use of Information systems and Information Technology, the receipt and issuance of inventories is done instantaneously, without human interaction. Therefore, those staff who were assigned to update bin cards can be utilized to perform other important duties within the organization.

12.2 Elimination of duplicated activities

Several employees may be doing the same or similar duties. However, with the use of Information Technology and Information Systems, many duplicated duties will be eliminated. For example, if employees at the various stores were required to update bin cards with receipt and issuance of inventories, then with the use of the software, inventories are updated at all locations, at the same time, without human interaction.

Another example can be seen in the use of a biometric attendance machine that captures employees' attendance data at all locations and transmits that information to the payroll. Once the data is uploaded through the software, leaders will just verify its accuracy, rather than inputting the data in the software.

12.3 Greater efficiency

Organizations who have invested in Information Technology and Information Systems have seen a reduction of work for employees, but also great efficiency. In the production plant, when some human duties are replaced by machines, there is greater consistency of output. Customers can be assured that they can purchase the same item and receive the same service or product at all times.

For example, those who want to acquire cupboards for their homes can now purchase them at a furniture store. Years ago, they would have had to solicit a joiner, and then that person would take some time to make cupboards for them. When those cupboards were made by hand, there were sometimes errors in the quality. However, since machines are now producing them, each customer will receive the same quality from the manufacturer.

13. Balancing of workload

Employees are sometimes burnt out because their workloads are not balanced. A few employees are carrying more work than they should, while others have lighter workloads. It may be difficult to always balance the workload of all employees, but it is expected that most employees will be given enough work for the organization to be productive.

13.1 What is to be done

Leaders must first identify what has to be done if they want to balance the workload. It may be important to determine what has to be done before deciding who will get it done. The work that has to be done for most organizations can be allocated by hours, days, weeks, months, etc.

13.2 Who is to do it

After it is determined what has to be done, then it becomes important to identify who will get it done. Leaders must ensure that they have an adequate number of employees to get the work done, or they can choose to outsource some of the tasks to an external person or organization if it is not feasible to complete the work internally.

13.3 When it has to be done

A great factor to consider is when the work has to be done. Once the timeline is known, then the same set of employees may get the work completed, or more employees may be required to participate in completing the work.

If short timelines are given to complete some tasks, then more resources must be assigned to complete the work. There are times when overtime work may be required to meet the timeline.

13.4 Prioritizing the work

When tasks are urgent, then there is a need to prioritize the work. While there are so many things to be done, all the work cannot be completed at once. Therefore, the tasks that have to be completed within the shortest possible time will be given more resources and attention.

If leaders do not prioritize the work, they may cause employees to become tired and probably frustrated. The lower level of employees may not be able to determine what is important and when those tasks have to be completed, so they depend on their leaders to make that determination for them. Leaders need to respect their subordinates and manage the workflow.

13.5 Who reviews the work

If work is completed without anyone reviewing it, errors can pass from the organization to the customers. While reviewing the work may appear to be a time-consuming task, it can reduce or eliminate any error in a good or service. When employees are too busy with their work, they may make mistakes and not have the time to recognize their errors. Oftentimes, whenever someone has to review the work of another person, the reviewer is able to detect errors before the product leaves the organization.

Even in mechanic shops, supervisors and managers will inspect the work done by the mechanics. These inspections are important, since it enables vehicles and machines to leave the mechanic shops free from errors that the mechanics caused.

13.6 What rest time may be given for some work

Leaders must factor in rest time as they balance the workload. Even some machines are expected to be rested and serviced.

Tasks that require little effort may be completed in the shortest possible time. However, some work will take months and years to complete. When the duration to complete the work is lengthy, leaders must consider rest time for employees. If employees are not provided with adequate rest, they will not be effective for the organization.

13.7 Are there sufficient resources to complete the work?

To balance the workload, there must be a determination of whether there are sufficient resources to complete the work. There may be a need for more people or machinery to complete the work. If the organization has enough resources, then it can proceed with the work. However, if there is a shortage of resources, then those resources must be made available to complete the work.

14. Workplace social events

Many business owners are concerned about maximizing their profits. While they want their profits to increase, they sometimes forget about the social life of their employees. For some employees, all they have known since working with the organization is work and more work. These employees may be away from the job whenever it is their vacation.

However, as business owners consider their profits, they must think about making their employees well balanced. They must consider some social events to help their employees to relax and interact with each other.

14.1 Celebration of birthdays and anniversaries

There are times when employers can pause some aspect of their operation just to celebrate their employees. For example, if the working hours for each day end at 16:30h, then if the employer is willing to make a sacrifice by allowing employees to finish work at 16:00h once per month to celebrate employees who have had birthdays that month, then many employees may feel appreciated. Some employers are willing to contribute towards their employees' birthday celebration and will provide meals for those who are celebrating their birthdays.

Other employers provide birthday and anniversary cards to their employees. These cards are often signed by the owner, managers, supervisor, and employees within that section. These little acknowledgments will motivate employees to feel relaxed and want to do more for the organization.

14.2 Celebration of newborn babies

Some employers will give employees time off to celebrate the new birth of their babies. When an employee has an addition to their family, some leaders will send a card to that employee to celebrate the addition to their family. These light gestures can mean so much to some employees and may allow them to take their minds off their work and relax.

14.3 Participating in bereavement

Now and again, employees will lose a loved one. Organizations may have a policy in place where compassionate leave will be granted to those employees. Some leaders will send a sympathy card or visit employees who lose a loved one.

14.4 Fun days and celebration of national holidays

At some organizations, they may observe holidays by having celebrations at the workplace. For these celebrations, management will sponsor the snacks and beverages. These celebrations can be done just before the lunch break or after the end of the working day. Many employees look forward to these celebrations. Sometimes, during these celebrations, employees get to know more about each other and also know more about their leaders.

A few dollars spent to celebrate employees can build great camaraderie among employees, which may cause some employees to be less stressed out.

14.5 Outdoor sports

Some employees have great abilities beyond the work they do for the organization. When employers organize outdoor sports, employees can showcase their great sportsmanship and sportswomanship. Before some employees started working with an organization, they were very active in sports, and they yearn for opportunities to demonstrate their sporting skills.

Those who are involved in sports may be provided with opportunities to prevent workplace burnout. Employers may organize sports among employees of the same department or across the organization, perhaps with competition among the divisions or branches of the organization.

14.6 Indoor sports

Some leaders will organize indoor sports for their employees, and some organizations have gyms and sporting facilities for employees to use. When some employees finish their day's work, they can utilize those facilities to keep themselves healthy and have a friendly competition among other employees.

These little interactions can be so meaningful to many employees. With these interactions, employees may have an avenue to burn out some of their emotions and be ready to deal with the challenges of work. Some work can be stressful, so they crave any opportunities to socialize with fellow employees.

15. Healthy workers

Employees should be reminded that they ought to consume a healthy diet, since their health is important for themselves and for their organization. Some organizations may have health charts and other signage to encourage employees to be healthy.

Many parents will remind their children to consume healthy meals. However, there are times when adults must also be reminded that they have to take care of their health.

15.1 Healthy diet

Some leaders will organize training sessions where presenters will encourage employees to eat certain foods which will make them healthy.

There are so many medications that persons can use to supplement any nutrients that are lacking. However, when persons learn which foods are nutritious for them, then they may make some adjustments to their diet. A balanced diet is important for everyone. Employees who are more involved in heavy labor-intensive work may be required to consume food with a higher proportion of nutrients that restores damaged cells and provides them with more energy.

Table 1. There are five main groups of nutrients

Main groups of nutrients	Explanation	Sources of the nutrients
Protein	The primary function of protein is to provide body-building or growth	Meat, fish, cheese, eggs,

	materials, so every cell in the body contains proteins.	wheat, rice, oats, beans
Fat (and oil)	Provides a convenient and concentrated source of energy, supplying more energy than the same weight of carbohydrate or protein.	Meat, butter, margarine, fish, nuts, fruits
Carbohydrate	Carbohydrates are the most important source of energy for the body. Almost all the cells of the body use glucose to distribute energy. Carbohydrate acts as a "protein sparer" so that protein can be used for its primary functions rather than as a source of energy.	Sugar, honey, molasses, jam, jelly, yam, sweet potato, breadfruit, rice, barley, corn

Vitamins	Vitamins are a group of chemical substances, most of which were identified during the 20th century as vital to the body. The body requires only small amounts of each vitamin. Vitamins can be classified according to the substances in which they dissolve.	Milk, cheese, eggs, carrot, spinach, watercress, cabbage, tomato, pumpkin, Callao, cod liver oil
Minerals	Bodybuilding. Control of bodily processes. Essential parts of body fluid. Some mineral elements are required in relatively large amounts.	Milk, cheese, broccoli, bok choy, legumes, bread

(Extract from Tull and Coward, 2009)

Some organizations may have a cafeteria for their employees that only sells food that will make employees healthy. The employer may subsidize the cafeteria to encourage employees to consume healthy meals regularly.

A balanced diet can reduce employees' sickness and tiredness. A balanced diet ensures that employees can continue to be productive to the organization as long as they remain with the organization, take some rest, and eat healthily.

With a balanced diet, employees must consume nutritious meals not just sometimes but daily or almost daily, if they can afford to do so. The human body needs to be nourished if it is going to be able to withstand the challenges of the organization.

15.2 Healthy body

The work some employees do will cause them to sit most of the day. Therefore, they need to exercise so that their blood will be circulated and they will exercise their muscles.

Some employers will acquire gym equipment for their employees. Some may charge employees a small fee to use the gym equipment, while others will make it free to their employees.

Within the gym area, there may be instructors who are there to guide employees on how to use the types of equipment. Some gym instructors may also encourage employees to consume a balanced diet.

15.3 No smoking and drinking of alcohol on the premises

Leaders are sometimes concerned about the health of their employees and also want to make sure that the employees are ready to contribute positively to the organization. So, some leaders will place signs around the organization to prohibit smoking and drinking of alcohol. These signs are there to help the employees and not to harm them. There may be other employees at the worksite who are not comfortable inhaling secondhand smoke.

When some employees consume alcohol, their behavior is not always accepted by others. Therefore, the leaders are only trying to help their employees to be healthy and be productive for the organization.

16. Medical insurance for employees

Please note that medical insurance does not prevent workplace burnout. However, some employees will become sick at work and need some additional support. Injuries can happen to employees as they work, so they look forward to some financial relief after their injuries. Workplace burnout can cause some employees to be on extended sick leave and have many medical bills. In those cases, medical insurance will be there to cushion the effect that some employees will experience during and after workplace burnout.

16.1 Joining medical insurance schemes

Some organizations may have medical insurance schemes for employees. If an organization does not have medical insurance, then employees should ask management about arranging for the organization to have a medical insurance scheme. Some leaders know the importance of medical insurance schemes for employees, so without employees asking them, those leaders will negotiate with an insurance company to provide this service to employees.

If employees recognize that the leaders of the organization do not want to arrange for a medical insurance scheme to be established, they can contact an insurance company to join a medical insurance scheme that they offer. With some insurance companies, if individuals approach them to join the medical insurance scheme, they will have to pay a higher premium.

Whatever option there is to join a medical insurance scheme, employees must seize the opportunity. When employees are sick from natural factors or are burnt out from work, they may need the benefits of the medical insurance scheme to recover some of the costs they incur for their recovery.

16.2 Insuring employees' families

Employees who have families must seek to have their family members on the medical insurance scheme. Many medical insurance schemes will give age limits for children to be included, and children who are above the age limit may not be allowed to be on their parents' medical coverage.

Those employees who have spouses and young children should have more of their family members included on the medical insurance scheme, as long as they are within the age limit. In the event of injuries to any family members, the principal person on the medical card does not have to work long hours to earn additional money to pay the medical bills for the family, as the medical coverage will allow each eligible family member to be covered and receive their medical benefits without any major additional cost.

16.3 Maximizing medical insurance options

Employees must consider taking maximum medical insurance options. For example, if they are allowed to seek coverage for optical service, dental, etc., then the employee should take all of those options. Each employee must work towards protecting their family in the event that they are unwell for a while. Sickness does not give people notice and does not consider someone's financial status before impacting them. Therefore, people need to protect themselves in whatever way they can.

Remember that while medical insurance cannot completely restore all damage that an employee may encounter due to workplace burnout, it may provide some comfort to the employee and their family. The money spent for medical insurance premiums cannot be compared with the benefits received.

Reference list

ACCA 2.1. (2000). *Information systems*. Foulks Lynch.

Noe, R. A., Hollenbeck, J. R., Gerhart, B., & Wright, P. M. (2015). *Human resource management: Gaining a competitive advantage* (9th ed.). McGraw-Hill Education.

Tull, A., & Coward, A. (2009). *Caribbean food and nutrition for CSEC*. Oxford University Press.

About the Author

Geary Reid has worked with multiple organizations, and he has seen workplace burnout among a number of employees. While employees strive to make a living for themselves, they sometimes push themselves too far and hurt their future. Reid has also seen some employers asking employees to do more and more, not taking into consideration that employees are humans and not machines. When good employees are pushed to their limits, they become tired and frustrated and then leave the organization, which often affects the organization's production.

Author Geary Reid is encouraging employers to take another look at the duties assigned to employees and to ensure that the employees have the resources to meet the organization's expectations. He also encourages employers to create work-life balance for their employees. As much as employers want more from employees, they ought to provide some social interaction for them. Establishing gyms at the workplace may be one way to prevent workplace burnout.

Reid believes in training employees so that they will become efficient in their duties. Employers must consider succession planning so that employees will become motivated, knowing that they may be considered for promotion sometime soon.

Over the years, author Geary Reid has spent time training subordinates to become better at their work. He also encourages employees to study to give themselves an opportunity to be promoted or to find an employer who will value their contribution. While Reid enjoys working hard and arriving at work before the required time, he tries to take time to have healthy discussions with employees about their social life and remind them to spend quality time with their families. He enjoys consuming healthy food regularly, including vegetables and fruits, and encourages employees to be healthy in order to prevent workplace burnout.

For some of the organizations he has worked with, Reid has often looked for ways to improve employees' performance by teaching them to be effective and also encouraging employers to acquire Information Technology and Information Systems to reduce employees' workload.

Reid often keeps his door to his office open so that employees will feel free to approach him and discuss any matters that are affecting them. He often shares solutions to their problems and encourages employees to do their best for their employers, but at the same time, he remembers that they are only human. He once again reminds employers to strike a balance between employees' work and their social life. Employees may not be able to do more for the organization if they are burnt out.

This page is intentionally left blank

This page is intentionally left blank

This page is intentionally left blank

This page is intentionally left blank

This page is intentionally left blank

This page is intentionally left blank